Presented to

_____

On This Day _____

From _____

Where were you, since the beginning of the world?
But now you are here, about me in every space,
room, sunlight, with your heart and arms and
the light of your soul.

—John Jay Chapman to his wife, Minna,
September 21, 1891

with
this
ring

with this
this
ring

promises to keep

JOANNA
WEAVER

WATERBROOK
PRESS

WITH THIS RING
PUBLISHED BY WATERBROOK PRESS
12265 Oracle Boulevard, Suite 200
Colorado Springs, Colorado 80921
A division of Random House Inc.

All Scripture quotations, unless otherwise indicated, are taken from the Holy Bible, New International Version®. NIV®. Copyright © 1973, 1978, 1984 by International Bible Society. Used by permission of Zondervan Publishing House. All rights reserved. Scripture quotations marked (KJV) are taken from the King James Version. Scripture quotations marked (TLB) are taken from The Living Bible, copyright © 1971. Used by permission of Tyndale House Publishers Inc., Wheaton, Illinois 60189. All rights reserved.

Every effort has been made to locate the copyright owners of the material used in this book. Please let us know if an error has been made, and we will make any necessary changes in subsequent printings.

ISBN 978-1-4000-7476-1

Published in association with the literary agency of Janet Kobobel Grant, Books & Such, 52 Mission Circle, Suite 122, PMB 170, Santa Rosa, CA 95409.

Library of Congress Cataloging-in-Publication Data
Weaver, Joanna.
   With this ring : promises to keep / Joanna Weaver. — 1st ed.
      p. cm.
   ISBN 978-1-4000-7476-1
1. Marriage—Religious aspects—Christianity. I. Title.
BV835.W3895 2008
265'.5—dc22

                              2007052389

Printed in the United States of America
2008—First Edition

10 9 8 7 6 5 4 3 2 1

SPECIAL SALES
Most WaterBrook Multnomah books are available in special quantity discounts when purchased in bulk by corporations, organizations, and special interest groups. Custom imprinting or excerpting can also be done to fit special needs. For information, please e-mail SpecialMarkets@WaterBrookMultnomah.com or call 1-800-603-7051.

To the Author of love
and
to my husband, John…
To be loved in such an all-encompassing, all-forgiving way
is beyond anything I deserve. I am forever grateful.

"My True Love Hath My Heart"

How can I write about you
When you are all the world?
When I know
That all that is good or just in me is only
An echo of you:
When all that I think is what you have breathed
on my heart:
And all I say
Although I am praised for it,
Is your book read aloud?

—Naomi Mitchison, *The Laburnum Branch,* 1926

Contents

Part Three: The Vows

Part Four: The Tokens

Part Five: The Declaration

You hold in your hands the book of my heart. I wrote it for those of you who are just now embarking on the great adventure called marriage. But it is written for married couples as well—from newlyweds to those married half a century or more. It is for all of us who, having once said, "I do," attempt daily to live out the brave promises we spoke in our wedding vows.

The inspiration behind *With This Ring* came from an unusual place. As a friend and I browsed through a local interior-design shop one day, we entered a room that featured a lovely bedroom ensemble. However, it was the calligraphy dancing just below the ceiling that caught my attention. Along the upper wall, an artist had hand-lettered the words of the traditional wedding vows in a lively mix of painted calligraphy and golden confetti: "Dearly beloved, we are gathered together here in the sight of God to join together this man and this woman in holy matrimony...."

"How beautiful," I told my friend as I circled the room, looking upward. "I would love to have this painted in our bedroom."

A loud snort of disgust interrupted my musings. Turning, I found a middle-aged man shaking his head with a sneer of amusement. "No one means those words anymore," he said.

Shocked, I replied, "Well, I do."

"Take it from me, sweetheart," he said, leaning in as if to let me in on a secret. "The men never do."

I could only stare at his self-satisfied grin as I pulled back in disbelief. To have a complete stranger be so openly cynical about marriage was new to me.

"Well, take it from me," I said when I finally found my voice. "My husband meant those words. And he proves it every day."

I went home shaken and saddened by the exchange, not because I am unaware of the challenges and disappointments marriage sometimes brings, but because the world so easily dismisses what God so highly values.

Out of that encounter at the design shop, however, came a determination to look deeper into the words we say so sincerely, though perhaps a bit naively, when we stand before God and family to become husband and wife. My search to find the meaning of the wedding tokens and traditions and the beauty surrounding them led to the writing of this book.

As you read this book and weave your own story into it,

I hope you will find the same inspiration and sense of wonder I experienced as I looked at the history and meaning behind the phrases of the wedding vows and the significance of the wedding ceremony. But even more, I hope you will walk away with the same holy determination to live out those vows daily in a deeper and more meaningful way than ever before.

From this day forward... Till death do us part.

Heart, are you
great enough
for a *love* that
never tires?

—ALFRED, LORD TENNYSON

Part One

The Betrothal Pledge

*Wilt thou have this woman
to be thy wedded wife?*

It all begins with a question: "Will you marry me?" One woman whispers, "Yes," while another declares, "You bet!" I know of one excited but jittery woman who punched her beau when he popped the question. When he finally came to, she was bending over him, repeating, "Yes, yes, yes, I'll marry you!"

In biblical times, the engagement was as solemn and important as the wedding ceremony is today. Rather than asking the girl himself (possibly fearing a left hook), a man or his representative approached the father of the woman he wanted to marry. If the father agreed, the two haggled through the bride price and other particulars. Once they came to an agreement, a date for the betrothal ceremony was set.

In a service separate from the actual wedding, the couple came, often meeting for the first time, to speak the binding words of the betrothal pledge. Rings were exchanged in the presence of witnesses and the promise sealed by a kiss. From that moment, the bride and groom were betrothed, an Old English word that means "for truth." They were bound to each other in an irreversible contract, although the marriage itself might not take place for several years. Each one signed the *ketubah,* an ornate legal document still used today in Jewish ceremonies. Only death or divorce could nullify the agreement.

Eventually the betrothal ceremony combined with the wedding, forming the marriage service we celebrate today. Marrying for love instead of money eliminated the need for matchmakers, middlemen, and elaborate legal documents. Though a ring is still given upon engagement, the ancient vows proclaiming the couple's free choice to marry aren't spoken till the day they wed.

When I think what life is,
and how seldom love is answered by love—
Marry him;
it is one of the moments
for which the world was made.

—E. M. FORSTER, *A ROOM WITH A VIEW*

Will You Be

I feel sad when I don't see you. Be married, why won't you? And come to live with me. I will make you as happy as I can. You shall not be obliged to work hard; and when you are tired, you may lie in my lap and I will sing you to rest. I will play you a tune upon the violin as often as you ask and as well as I can; and leave off smoking, if you say so.... I would always be very kind to you, I think, because I love you so well. I will not make you bring in wood and water, or feed the pig, or milk the cow, or go to the neighbours to borrow milk. Will you be married?

Letter from a suitor in
nineteenth-century America

Married?

My wife would have blond hair and green eyes. She'd be funny but serious sometimes. She'd be smart, pretty, and nice. We would go to parties once a month and go to baseball games. We would especially have fun. She'd give me a kiss every day and love me. She'd listen when I talk. She would brag about me a little. We would spend ten minutes talking to each other each day. We would have three children, Bobby, Amy, and Rick. She would be my best friend.

Boy, age 11, from
Take Time to Play Checkers

"Love Comes Quietly"

Love comes quietly,
finally, drops
about me, on me,
in the old ways.

What did I know
thinking myself
able to go
alone all the way.

—Robert Creeley

Giving the Bride Away

According to romantic legend, Helene, the beautiful daughter of Maximilian II, king of Germany in the sixteenth century, was once courted by two suitors. When she was unable to choose between the handsome German baron and the dashing Spaniard, the two proposed a duel for her hand, but the prospective father-in-law suggested a less-deadly contest. Handing each man a gunnysack, the king promised to give his daughter in marriage to the first man who could bag the other.

After wrestling nearly an hour, Baron von Talbert finally succeeded in stuffing his opponent into the bag. He lifted the bulging sack and carried it across the room. Dropping it at Helene's feet, the baron made his proposal, which was immediately accepted by the fair maiden.

Helene was one of the lucky ones—she could accept or reject her suitor. In more primitive times, a man didn't bother asking for a pretty girl's hand in marriage. He just took it. The honeymoon is said to have evolved from the need to hide from the angry fathers and brawny brothers of kidnapped brides. After a month or so, the newlywed couple came out of hiding. The groom made a payment suitable for the loss of a daughter, thus appeasing his offended in-laws and allowing him and his blushing bride to get on with happily ever after.

The marriage-by-capture approach faded as civilization grew, and "Me Tarzan, you Jane" gave way to "Father knows best." Arranged marriages took center stage with many anxious parents betrothing their children while still in the cradle. It wasn't until the tenth century that women gained the right to choose their husbands according to their own judgment. Yet the approval of parents was important, just as it is today.

When my husband-to-be approached my father for permission to marry me, there were no other suitors begging for my hand and so, sadly, no need for a wrestling match. I've been told the conversation went something like this: "I'd like to ask for your daughter's hand in marriage," John said. "But if you don't mind, I'd like the rest of her as well!"

Legally, John didn't need my parents' permission to marry me. But in honoring my father, he honored me, opening a door of loving communication and support that remains today. We received their blessing, a gift which was and is priceless to me. In their approval, I found God's confirmation and the assurance that this was no guessing game. I'd truly captured the right man for me.

And I didn't even need a gunnysack.

Laban and Bethuel answered, "This is from the
LORD.... Here is Rebekah; take her and go, and let
her become the wife of your master's son, as the
LORD has directed."...

   ...So they called Rebekah and asked her, "Will
you go with this man?"

   "I will go," she said.

   —Genesis 24:50–51, 58

God's Surprise

There is no surprise more magical than the surprise
of being loved: It is God's finger on man's shoulder.

—⁓— Charles Morgan

God brought you to me, sweet lover, and I think He
raised me to be of use to you.

—⁓— Christine de Pisan

I never thought I could love anything without four
wheels and a stick shift.

—⁓— Michael McFarlane

Tape here a memento from when you became engaged or from one of your favorite recent dates—a ticket stub, a picture, a menu, a flower, a snippet of wrapping paper from the engagement-ring box.

Grow old along with me!
The best is yet to be,
The last of life, for which
the first was made:
Our times are in his hand.

—Robert Browning, "Rabbi Ben Ezra"

"A Marriage"

You are holding up a ceiling
with both arms. It is very heavy,
but you must hold it up, or else
it will fall down on you. Your arms
are tired, terribly tired,
and, as the day goes on, it feels
as if either your arms or the ceiling
will soon collapse.

But then,
unexpectedly,
something wonderful happens:
Someone,
a man or a woman,
walks into the room
and holds their arms up
to the ceiling beside you.

So you finally get
to take down your arms.
You feel the relief of respite,
the blood flowing back
to your fingers and arms.
And when your partner's arms tire,
you hold up your own
to relieve him again.

And it can go on like this
for many years
without the house falling.

—Michael C. Blumenthal

The Day Love Was Born

The angels saw it all. Creator spoke, and suddenly the dark, swirling chaos of the cosmos disappeared, leaving an ordered universe in its place.

Night. Day. Land. Water. Word by word, day by day, the plan of Creator unfolded before the heavenly host, each creation more wonderful than the last. The Father spoke. The Spirit moved. And the angels applauded.

"Marvelous!" cried one angel. "Incredible!" said another.

The brilliant blue and green planet beckoned with beauty, nestled against the black night sprinkled with stars. Layered with lush forests and soaring mountains, it was a palace fit for a King. As though God himself would dwell there.

"Unthinkable!" cried one. "Ludicrous!" said another.

And yet it was so. Each evening Creator left his throne and walked in the garden he'd created, visiting the man he'd formed from the dust of this new world. The man created to fellowship with almighty God.

Why? the angels wondered. Never had such an honor been given. And yet somehow they understood. The heart of Creator was so large it ached to love. The adoration of angels and their unrestrained praise filled his ears but failed to touch his heart. He longed for love. Not worship. Not fearful reverence. But love.

Laughter echoed across the garden and into heaven. The fellowship was sweet. Creator smiled as Created named each animal, exulting in every one. Together they explored the secrets of Eden and the wonder of this new friendship. But as the days passed, a growing conviction gripped the heart of Creator. A bittersweet realization that there was still more to give.

Each creature had a mate. Another of its kind. But the man was alone.

"It is not good for man to be alone. I will make a help-mate." And in that moment love was born. Not in the creation of the woman, but in the Creator's willingness to share the man. In the Creator's willingness to give.

For God so loved…he gave. Though it meant sacrificing the single-minded devotion of the man, God gave. Though it meant sharing the communion meant only for him, God gave. Though it meant the willful disobedience of man and woman would someday cost Creator the life of his dear Son, God gave.

We, too, must give if we endeavor to love. Love holds no room for selfishness. It is only in laying down our life that we find it. It is only in losing that we win.

We can learn a lot from the day love was born.

Do nothing out of selfish ambition or vain conceit,
but in humility consider others better than yourselves.
    —Philippians 2:3

I have nothing to share with you but my life.

⚜ Peter McWilliams

He poured so gently and naturally into my life, like batter into a bowl of batter, honey into a jar of honey. The clearest water sinking into sand.

⚜ Justine Sydney

My life has been the awaiting you,
Your footfall was my own heart's beat.

⚜ Paul Valéry

Look for a sweet person. Forget rich.

⚜ Estée Lauder

In marriage
we marry a mystery, an other,
a counterpart.
In a sense the person we marry
is a stranger about whom we have
a magnificent hunch.

—Daphne Rose Kingma

What qualities first drew you to your spouse?

_____

_____

_____

_____

_____

_____

_____

_____

_____

_____

_____

_____

_____

_____

_____

_____

_____

_____

_____

What was your proposal like? Was it a surprise?

_____

_____

_____

_____

_____

_____

_____

_____

_____

_____

_____

_____

_____

_____

_____

_____

_____

_____

_____

_____

How did you tell other people the news of your engagement?

_____

_____

_____

_____

_____

_____

_____

_____

_____

_____

_____

_____

_____

_____

_____

_____

_____

_____

_____

_____

Part Two

The Ceremony

I take thee to be my wedded husband,
to have and to hold
from this day forward…

She walks toward him in quiet beauty. His destiny, his life, all wrapped up in this woman soon to be his wife. The music softens, and his anxiety fades as he looks into her face, full of serenity. And in that single moment he knows—this is right. Like a wandering stream finally reaching the sea, his heart has finally found a resting place.

It isn't enough for a couple to say, "I love you." It isn't enough simply to live together. A love like this cannot be contained in a cardboard box, which disintegrates with time and disinterest. This love is too precious. This love requires the golden chalice of commitment. This love requires a ceremony—a sacred assembly of all those we know, called to witness and hold us accountable to all we say. Before God and humankind, we speak holy vows—pounding earthly stakes to form new boundaries and open new territory. From this day forward, we are one till death do us part.

The veil, the tuxedo, the flowers—they make up the wedding. Patience, kindness, gentleness—they make up the marriage.

For where two or three are gathered together in my name, there am I in the midst of them.

    —Matthew 18:20, KJV

Gathered Together

Dearly beloved, we are gathered together here
in the sight of God,
and in the face of this company
to join together, this man and this woman
in holy matrimony;
which is…commended of Saint Paul
to be honorable among all men:
and therefore is not by any
to be entered into unadvisedly or lightly;
but reverently, discreetly, advisedly, soberly,
and in the fear of God.
Into this holy estate these two persons present
come now to be joined.
If any man can show just cause
why they may not lawfully be joined together,
let him now speak, or else hereafter
forever hold his peace.

—The Book of Common Prayer

Come What May

Kim Carpenter had never seen anything more beautiful in his life. The day he had waited for was finally here. Teal ribbon and pink roses lined the candlelit chapel where he and two hundred fifty guests stood. But Kim saw only his bride. A stab of pure joy pierced his heart as Krickitt met him at the altar, her incredible blue eyes mirroring the excitement and love in his own eyes.

Every detail of the ceremony is seared into Kim's memory. The words he spoke to Krickitt were broken by emotion and filled with love. "I will love, comfort, and cherish you…"

Of that day several years ago Krickitt remembers nothing. It isn't a case of bridal jitters or excitement overload. The wedding is gone—wiped from the keepsake book of Krickitt's memory by the nearly fatal car crash she and Kim were in just ten weeks after their wedding. Eighteen months of Krickitt's life before the wedding and four months after have disappeared into the mist of a coma and brain injury. Gone as well are the memories of her and Kim's courtship, love, and marriage.

Kim hardly recognized his wife, "she was so messed up." Though he had several injuries of his own, he drove through the night to the hospital to which his wife had been airlifted.

As he held her pale, limp hand, he whispered, "Hang in there, babe. We're going to get through this."

The doctors put Krickitt's chance of survival at less than 1 percent, but people began to pray. Ten days after the accident, Krickitt started to regain consciousness. Kim watched anxiously as his wife emerged from the foggy coma.

"What year is it?" the nurse asked three weeks after the accident.

"Nineteen sixty-five." She was three decades off.

Other questions followed. Some Krickitt answered right, others wrong. But there was one question Kim wasn't sure he wanted answered.

"Who's your husband?"

Krickitt paused a moment, then said, "I'm not married."

It was a blow Kim will never forget.

After many months Krickitt finally moved home, and she and Kim began the process of reassembling their lives. But nothing was the same. "So, how did I do this 'wife thing'?" Krickitt asked. "Did I cook dinner? Did I make you a lunch?"

"I felt more like Krickitt's father than her husband," Kim says. "We had to start over." And start over they did. They began dating again. He had wooed her once, and Kim was determined to win her again. "I had said my vows before God—'in sickness and in health'—and I meant them."

As for Krickitt, Kim was just a man in a wedding photograph who stood beside a woman who looked like her. "But I knew that if I loved him before, God could help me love him again."

Kim's plan began to work. They spent Saturday afternoons at the lake together, cutting across whitecaps on Wave-Runners, then whiled away the evenings laughing and talking about the day over pizza—Canadian bacon. Romantic dinners and strolling through Wal-Mart hand in hand initiated a new legacy of love. Krickitt found herself thinking how

Two and a half years ago, I made a vow before God, and as I stated then, I state now with greater love and desire. I promise to defend our love and hold it in highest regard. I promise to be forgiving, understanding, and patient. I promise to tend to your every need. I promise to respect and honor you fully.

—KIM CARPENTER

AT HIS SECOND WEDDING CEREMONY

she'd miss him if he were gone. As for Kim—well, he certainly wasn't feeling like her father anymore.

On Valentine's Day two years after the accident, Kim proposed once again. Krickitt accepted.

The ceremony was simple yet sacred. The tiny log chapel in the Sangre de Cristo mountains near their New Mexico home was filled with close friends and relatives. Their faces lit only by lanterns, Kim looked into the beautiful blue eyes of the woman he loved. Then, each after the other, they repeated the vows that had held them together. Vows that had been tested by fire and found true.

To new couples and to those about to be married, Kim and Krickitt Carpenter offer this advice: "Read your vows carefully. Repeat them twenty times. Look between the lines, understand the promises you make. Fill in the spaces with every possibility, and then, if you're ready, say them. But know this: You may be called to live them out in ways you never imagined."

A Place to Rest

Here all seeking is over,
the lost has been found,
a mate has been found
to share the chills of winter—
now Love asks
that you be united.
Here is a place to rest,
a place to sleep,
a place in heaven.
Now two are becoming one,
the black night is scattered,
the eastern sky grows bright.
At last the great day has come!

—Hawaiian song

The Wonder of It All

It was a match made in heaven. It had to be. For a man like John to choose to spend his life with a woman like me, well, it seemed miraculous.

For a split moment, I wondered if it was all some marvelous mirage. There I stood, in my childhood church, marrying my childhood dream. I'd met John when I was thirteen. So tall and handsome, he was everything I'd ever hoped for. But, alas, he was nearly four years older, and as everyone knows, sixteen-year-olds-going-on-seventeen-year-olds never look at thirteen-year-olds. So I worshiped from afar. He was the sun, the moon, the stars, and I, the earthbound mole.

Then one day, when I was sixteen going on seventeen, some kind of holy chemistry erupted between us, and I knew he was the one. He agreed. Three years later we stood at the altar.

"Will you take this woman to be your wedded wife?" The question hung in the air like gossamer stretched thin between us. A sudden terror rose in my throat. What if he said no? What if this was some cruel dream and I suddenly awoke to darkness?

But then, like a soft, silken ribbon, his gaze caught mine and pulled me in. There was no fear in his eyes, no doubt, no double-mindedness. Only a tender determination. And tears. In the sparkling blue depths of his eyes, I caught a glimpse of all that I could be—a reflection of what he saw when he looked at me. His choice was no cosmic fluke. This man loved me. Me.

Wedded wife. The word *wed* comes from the same root word as *wage*. It goes back to the tradition of the bride price.

> *He's more myself than I am.*
> *Whatever our souls are made of,*
> *his and mine are the same....*
> *If all else perished, and he remained,*
> *I should still continue to be;*
> *and if all else remained,*
> *and he were annihilated,*
> *the universe would turn*
> *to a mighty stranger....*
> *He's always, always in my mind;*
> *not as a pleasure...,*
> *but as my own being.*

—EMILY BRONTË, *WUTHERING HEIGHTS*

When a man wanted to marry a woman, he was required to pay a certain amount of money or goods prescribed by her father. The more desirable the woman, the higher the price.

There's always a price to pay when you love. And I'm afraid there have been times in our decades of marriage when John has paid dearly. Times when what I could be contrasts painfully with what I am. And yet, he continues to love me. Me.

The tender strands of his love embrace me. They constrain me, refusing to let me go. They uphold me when I'm weary of trying to stand. "She belongs to me," they say. "She is my wedded wife."

Tape or write here memories from planning your wedding ceremony—pictures, lists you made, music, questions for the pastor, Bible verses that became the focus of the service…

_____

_____

_____

_____

_____

_____

_____

_____

_____

_____

I love you so much
and so completely that now I
believe in marriage. You must be more
than mine—you must be mysteriously,
and legally, and eternally, and respectably,
mine. If there were no marriage service,
my instinct would invent it.

—John Oliver Hobbes, *The Dream and the Business*

A Dream Come True

It had never seemed right to Jim Porter. A woman like Patty deserved all the frills and lace little girls dream of in a wedding. Instead, they had been married in a simple ceremony with four friends looking on. Patty had worn a borrowed wedding gown. There was no fancy reception. For years Jim had dreamed of making their twenty-fifth anniversary the wedding they never had. But Lou Gehrig's disease changed all that.

The doctors told Jim he had six to twelve months to live. Lou Gehrig's is a degenerative nervous system disorder without any cure, a mixture of pain and paralysis that in 80 percent of cases leads to death within two years.

But Jim Porter beat the odds. Two years later he was still alive. And so was his dream.

Without Patty knowing, Jim began piecing together a tribute to the woman he loved so much. For someone in perfect health, a wedding is a giant undertaking. But Jim refused to let his trembling hands and increasing paralysis stop him.

When he and his teenage daughters couldn't find bridesmaids' dresses they liked, Jim traded a copier for his sister's sewing machine and sewed the off-the-shoulder, burgundy satin dresses himself. To his sister's amazement, his seams were nearly perfect.

Never mind the fact Jim Porter had never sewn in his life. "I knew there was a talent," he jokes.

Flowers. Music. A cake. A photographer. Jim had thought

That I may come near to her,
draw me nearer to Thee than to her;
That I may know her,
make me to know Thee more than her;
That I may love her with the perfect love
of a perfectly whole heart,
cause me to love Thee more than her
and most of all.
Amen. Amen.
That nothing may be between me and her,
be Thou between us, every moment.
That we may be constantly together,
draw us into separate loneliness with Thyself.
And when we meet breast to breast,
my God, let it be on Thy own.
Amen. Amen.

—Temple Gairdner

of everything. Even Patty's dress. He and the girls shopped for months looking for the perfect gown. Jim unveiled all his plans the night before their twenty-fourth anniversary.

"I have no guarantee I will be around next year," Jim explained to Patty, who was overwhelmed by the extent of his love and the detail of his planning. "My only disappointment is that I didn't get to make your wedding gown."

The following evening Jim and Patty Porter stood together in gentle candlelight. Friends and family watched through tears as Jim and Patty exchanged the vows they'd first spoken so many years before. The ceremony was hushed and holy, yet filled with joy.

"The whole thing was such a picture of Jim's love for me," Patty says. "And yet it wasn't a surprise. He's been loving me like this for twenty-four years." Jim Porter had created the crowning moment of the years of cherishing the woman God had given him.

Here he is, Patty thought as she gazed at Jim through a mist of veil and tears, *loving me again!*

Rituals are important. Nowadays it's not hip to be married. I'm not interested in being hip.

 John Lennon

May heaven grant you in all things your heart's desire— husband, house, and a happy, peaceful home; for there is nothing better in this world than that man and wife should be of one mind in a house. It discomfits their enemies, makes the hearts of their friends glad, and they themselves know more about it than anyone.

John Lennon

Homer, *The Odyssey*

An ideal wife is any woman who has an ideal husband.

Booth Tarkington

I do love you so—it's like a well, so deep that if you went to the very bottom, you would see stars.

Victoria Sackville-West

Chains do not hold a marriage together. It is threads, hundreds of tiny threads which sew people together through the years.

Simone Signoret

Why are the marriage ceremony and vows important to you?

_____

_____

_____

_____

_____

_____

_____

_____

_____

_____

_____

_____

_____

_____

_____

_____

_____

_____

_____

_____

_____

Describe some memorable moments from your wedding
ceremony. What was your favorite part?

_____

_____

_____

_____

_____

_____

_____

_____

_____

_____

_____

_____

_____

_____

_____

_____

_____

_____

_____

In what ways does your spouse show you his love?

_____

_____

_____

_____

_____

_____

_____

_____

_____

_____

_____

_____

_____

_____

_____

_____

_____

_____

_____

_____

Part Three

The Vows

For better for worse, for richer for poorer,
in sickness and in health,
to love and to cherish, till death do us part,
according to God's holy ordinance.
And thereto I pledge my faith.

Simple phrases. "I do" spoken twice. A lifetime of promise within two tiny words. And with these words we write the opening sentence of our marriage. Side by side, hand in hand, we declare in bold strokes our single-hearted allegiance: "This is my love—there will be no other."

Over the centuries, millions of couples have committed themselves to each other using the traditional wedding ceremony found in the Book of Common Prayer. Whether spoken in a chapel or whispered on a hillside, these vows are sacred words. Powerful promises. They are not to be spoken lightly nor abandoned when the going gets tough. So help us God.

Phrase by phrase, promise upon promise, we write a covenant linking our life with another. Will you? Can you? Do you? The answer comes as sure as the sunrise, bursting through our hearts and dancing out into the sacred space where we stand: Yes, I will. I can. And I do!

Historically, marriage vows were irrevocable. Once spoken, they were never to be broken. Those who dared go back on their word paid dearly, even to death. While vows may have lost their potency in today's fickle society, they still echo in the heavenlies. As God is our witness, we will be called to give account for every word we've spoken.

"I pronounce you man and wife. You may kiss your bride." These are the final words of the ceremony and the first words of our life together. The next page lies bare. And in our hands, we hold the pen.

Whatever your lips utter you must be sure to do, because you made your vow freely to the LORD your God with your own mouth.

—Deuteronomy 23:23

The Love Chapter

If I had the gift of being able to speak in
        other languages without learning them,
and could speak in every language there is
        in all of heaven and earth,
but didn't love others, I would only be
        making noise.
If I had the gift of prophecy
        and knew all about what is going to
        happen in the future,
knew everything about *everything*, but didn't
        love others, what good would it do?
Even if I had the gift of faith so that I could
        speak to a mountain and make it move,
I would still be worth nothing at all without
        love.
If I gave everything I have to poor people,
        and if I were burned alive for preaching
        the Gospel but didn't love others,
it would be of no value whatever.
Love is very patient and kind, never jealous
        or envious,

never boastful or proud, never haughty or
      selfish or rude.
Love does not demand its own way.
It is not irritable or touchy.
It does not hold grudges and will hardly
      even notice when others do it wrong.
It is never glad about injustice, but rejoices
      whenever truth wins out.
If you love someone you will be loyal to
      him no matter what the cost.
You will always believe in him, always
      expect the best of him,
and always stand your ground in defending
      him.
All the special gifts and powers from God
      will someday come to an end,
but love goes on forever.

—1 Corinthians 13:1–8, TLB

Describe your greatest dream for your marriage.

_____

_____

_____

_____

_____

_____

_____

_____

_____

_____

_____

_____

_____

_____

_____

_____

A happy marriage
is a long conversation that
always seems too short.

—André Maurois

A Strong Foundation

Building a marriage is like building a house: you must begin with a strong foundation. Before you can hammer and nail or prep and paint, you must pour cement footings. Unseen when the house is finished, these underground footings keep your home secure.

In earthquake-plagued California, the building codes require even more. When one church set out to build a new sanctuary, they discovered they couldn't simply pour a slab of concrete. For months they had to drill holes thirty feet deep into the earth, down to bedrock. After placing steel rebars inside, they filled the holes with tons of cement. Finally they were ready to pour the slab that would form the floor of their new building. All that work—all that money!—for something no one could see and no one would notice. Until the next "Big One," that is.

When the earth shakes, it's better to have your footings on solid rock than on shifting sand. As the children's church song says, we need to be wise. Because you can count on one thing in this life: the rains are going to come. Your earth will eventually tremble, and your house had better stand.

Wedding vows are pilings that reach down to the bedrock of integrity in our lives. Like concrete and rebar, they anchor the visible to the unshakable. They are simple promises, made of rock and mud and fire-driven steel. But when we pour the foundation of our future upon them, our marriage may shift but it won't fall.

These are not easy promises. It's no mistake that *maturity* and *matrimony* come from the same Latin word. As Joseph Barth said, "Marriage is our last, best chance to grow up."

These are not ordinary promises. They marry earth and heaven. For when we pledge our fidelity to each other, God stands as witness to our words. And he doesn't take his job lightly.

When you make a vow to God, do not delay in fulfilling it. He has no pleasure in fools; fulfill your vow. It is better not to vow than to make a vow and not fulfill it.

—Ecclesiastes 5:4–5

Endless Forgiveness

Love is an act of endless forgiveness, a tender look which becomes a habit.

Peter Ustinov

It is a little embarrassing that, after forty-five years of research and study, the best advice I can give to people is to be a little kinder to each other.

Aldous Huxley

A happy marriage is the union of two good forgivers.

Ruth Bell Graham

May You Have Enough

May you have enough happiness to
    keep you sweet,
Enough trials to keep you strong,
Enough sorrow to keep you human,
Enough hope to keep you happy,
Enough failure to keep you humble,
Enough success to keep you eager,
Enough friends to give you comfort,
Enough faith and courage in yourself
    to banish depression,
Enough wealth to meet your needs,
Enough determination to make each
    day a better day than yesterday.

—Unknown author

Love is not a possession but a growth.
The heart is a lamp with just oil enough
    to burn for an hour,
and if there be no oil to put in again,
    its light will go out.
God's grace is the oil that fills the lamp of love.

—Henry Ward Beecher

To Have and to Hold

For forty-six years, Cliff has carried the scrap of paper on which his "Yakima Peach" wrote her name and number the day they met, carefully laminated and readily available. To all who will listen, he recounts the story of their meeting and the marvelous gift God gave him when his sweet Annette said, "I do." The voice of the tall, lanky, former dump-truck driver catches with emotion and his eyes grow misty when he speaks of his tiny bride.

I've lived surrounded by Cliff and Annette's love. A love that goes beyond "to have" and embraces "to hold." Each evening, as far back as I can remember, my father has held my mother in a blue velvet rocker. Sometimes they talk. Sometimes they pray. Sometimes they simply hold each other, whispering things without speaking a word.

Early on, my siblings and I loved to interrupt their kisses and caresses, eager for some of the affection so tangible in our home. Mom would laugh as Daddy reached down and picked us up, piling us one upon the other until we were a pyramid of little arms and legs all tangled up in their love. Then we'd rock in the dusky hours of early evening. Laughing and telling stories. Loving and being loved.

I have been given a rich dowry of demonstrative love. I've

received the gift of touch. The shelter of an embrace. I've witnessed the joy of a kiss. The strength found when two people meet, then turn to face whatever comes, hand in hand.

Some nights when it's cold and dark and the fear of tomorrow claws at my throat, choking all hope, I reach for my husband. "Just hold me," I beg. Something mysterious happens as I lie wrapped in his love—a transfer of strength. I can't explain it. The words that come to mind seem too trivial on one hand, too mystical on the other.

I only know what it means to me. Secure in my husband's love, surrounded by his prayers, and safe in his arms, I surrender to sleep, knowing I'm not alone.

So much is lost when we settle for "to have" and miss the "to hold."

We are each of us angels
with only one wing.
And we can only fly
embracing each other.

—LUCIANO DE CRESCENZO

A Program for Happiness

To live content with small means;
To seek elegance rather than luxury,
and refinement rather than fashion;
To be worthy, not respectable,
and wealthy, not rich;
To study hard, think quietly,
talk gently, act frankly;
To listen to the stars and birds,
to babies and sages, with an open heart;
To bear all cheerfully, do all bravely,
await occasions, hurry never.
In a word, to let the spiritual, unbidden
    and unconscious,
grow up through the common.

—William Henry Channing

Transforming Love

Have you ever seen transforming love?

I have. I've seen it in my parents' lifelong infatuation with each other, and I saw it again many years ago in an elderly couple on a warm September evening after church choir practice.

Jean was a gray-haired woman who sang alto. Quiet and unassuming, she tended to blend into the background. She came and went, sang and left. I guess I never truly saw Jean until the day I met her husband, Al, as he picked her up from choir. From that moment, my perception of Jean was forever altered.

"Isn't she something?" Al said, nudging me with an elbow as he smiled and winked at his bride of thirty years. "That woman brings me so much joy."

Pale, quiet Jean did something I would never have expected. She blushed. Al went on applauding her attributes, building her up with his words. And she began to blossom. Right there before my eyes.

A prolific poet, Al asked if he could quote me a poem about his wife, and I said, "Of course! You must!"

"Oh, Al…," she muttered, embarrassed yet pleased.

I don't remember the words of his poem, but the beauty

I saw unfold from deep within Jean I shall never forget. It changed the lowly alto into a glowing madonna and one of the most beautiful women I've ever seen.

Transforming love. The kind that lasts despite time and age. The kind that sticks around when we're not as wonderful as we could be or should be.

The kind of love that still softly glows, though her lover and his poems have since been silenced by the ravages of Alzheimer's disease. In the three short years since I'd seen them last, Jean's vibrant husband had disappeared, leaving an empty shell. My eyes filled with tears as I expressed my sympathy and how hard it must be.

"It's not hard to love," Jean told me, bending down to tuck in a lap quilt around the emaciated legs of her beloved Al. She kissed him softly on the cheek. "Not when you've been loved like I've been loved."

Love seems the swiftest,
but it is the slowest of all growths.
No man or woman really knows
what perfect love is
until they have been married
a quarter of a century.

—Mark Twain

"Love"

I love you,
Not only for what you are
But for what I am
When I am with you.

I love you,
Not only for what
You have made of yourself
But for what
You are making of me.

I love you,
For the part of me
That you bring out;

I love you,
For putting your hand
Into my heaped-up heart
And passing over
All the foolish, weak things

That you can't help
Dimly seeing there,
And for drawing out
Into the light
All the beautiful belongings
That no one else had looked
Quite far enough to find.

I love you because you
Are helping me to make
Of the lumber of my life
Not a tavern
But a temple;
Out of the works
Of my every day
Not a reproach
But a song.

—Roy Croft

Stirring the

Stirring the oatmeal is a humble act.... It represents a
willingness...to find meaning in the simple, unromantic
tasks: earning a living, living within a budget, putting
out the garbage.

Robert A. Johnson

You can never be happily married to another until
you get a divorce from yourself. Successful marriage
demands a certain death to self.

Jerry McCant

Oatmeal

To repress a harsh answer, to confess a fault, and to stop (right or wrong) in the midst of self-defense, in gentle submission, sometimes requires a struggle like life and death; but these *three* efforts are the golden threads with which domestic happiness is woven.

Caroline Gilman

Let Me Be Your Mirror

On their honeymoon, Bill and Pam Farrel were preparing for an evening out. Bill was ready and waiting for Pam. He lay on the hotel bed, content, watching his lovely new wife fuss with her hair and congratulating himself on his good taste in women. When Pam began to criticize her physical attributes, nothing Bill said seemed to comfort her.

"Inside I was becoming frustrated," Bill writes in their book *Love to Love You!* "After all, she was criticizing my wife!

"I got up and walked toward Pam. I wrapped my arms around her and gave her a reassuring hug. Then I stepped back, took her face tenderly in my hands, and said, 'Pam, let me be your mirror. You are gorgeous! Let me reflect back to you the beautiful woman you are. If we have to throw all the mirrors in our house away, we will. From now on, I will be your mirror!'"

That is the gift we bring to marriage when we bring the very best love—the purest Godlike, love-your-wife-as-Christ-loves-the-church love. It is in the mirror of forever love that we see ourselves and each other most clearly. Both the good and the bad.

We offer unconditional acceptance, resisting the urge to change or manipulate each other. Gently, honestly, we peel away our own masks, revealing weaknesses and vulnerabilities. Then with tender hands we reach to cover each other's oh-so-visible imperfections with love.

And we whisper, "Let me be your mirror. Let me reflect back to you the beauty of who you are."

Your embraces alone
give life to my heart.

—ANCIENT EGYPTIAN INSCRIPTION

Marriage is no joke; it is not like rice which can be spat out if it is too hot.

Philippine proverb

Knit your hearts with an unslipping knot.

William Shakespeare

In a successful marriage, there is no such thing as one's way. There is only the way of both, only the bumpy, dusty, difficult, but always mutual path!

Phyllis McGinley

In what ways has your mate's love changed the way you view yourself?

_____

_____

_____

_____

_____

_____

_____

_____

_____

_____

_____

_____

_____

_____

_____

_____

_____

_____

_____

In what ways do "opposites attract" in your relationship? How do your differences complement each other?

_____

_____

_____

_____

_____

_____

_____

_____

_____

_____

_____

_____

_____

_____

_____

_____

_____

_____

_____

_____

Describe a marriage you've seen that exemplifies how you want to live out your own wedding vows.

_____

_____

_____

_____

_____

_____

_____

_____

_____

_____

_____

_____

_____

_____

_____

_____

_____

_____

_____

_____

Part Four

The Tokens

With this ring I thee wed
and with all my worldly goods
I thee endow.

From the earliest days, a ring has been used to seal important or sacred agreements. The unending circle symbolizes the unending love we bring to marriage.

The first known use of a finger ring in a marriage ceremony was in the Third Dynasty of the Old Kingdom of Egypt around 2800 BC. The Egyptians believed that the circle, having no end or beginning, symbolized eternity—which signified how long the marriage was binding.

The ring, or the "joining of hands" in some form, appears in nearly all cultures and all ages as a symbol of covenant. Hindu priests bind the bride's and groom's hands with grass. In ancient Ireland a man gave the girl he wanted to marry a bracelet woven of human hair. Before the advent of rings in Jewish marriages, a coin was broken in two, and one half was given to the bride and the other to the groom as a symbol of the husband's ability to care for his wife financially. The Romans often gave their brides a heavy iron ring with the keys to their house strung upon it—"with all my worldly goods I thee endow."

As time went by, rings were made of many different materials. Peasants often wove wedding bands from hemp, while other cultures formed rings from leather, carved stone, and crude metals. Gold was a favorite choice of the more affluent, because of its beauty and durability.

The first known use of a Christian pledge-ring was in AD 860. Usually gold and without decoration, it was often engraved with the bride's and groom's names, a tradition that still continues today. Abraham Lincoln had Mary Todd's wedding ring engraved with "Love is Eternal." Another romantic husband engraved in his beloved's ring: "Each for the other, both for God. MWG to MEH October 21, 1890."

The wedding ring is worn on the left hand, a tradition begun by the Greeks. They believed a major artery ran from the heart straight to the fourth finger of the left hand. While that idea has been disproved by modern science, it is a lovely reminder of the commitment we make to love.

This ring is round and hath no end,
So is my love unto my friend.

—Sixteenth-century verse

In an ancient church ritual, the ring was placed first on the thumb, "in the name of the Father"; next on the forefinger, "and of the Son"; then on the middle finger, "and of the Holy Spirit." It was placed last on the third finger, "Amen," and left there as a seal of the marriage bond. An outward manifestation of an inward choice, the ring circles not only our finger but also our heart.

You have been such light to me that other women have
been your shadows.

Wendell Berry

Flesh of thy flesh, bone of thy bone,
I here, though there, yet both but one.

Anne Bradstreet

Remember this…that very little is needed to make
a happy life.

Marcus Aurelius

So Very

I got a thick letter from Ruth postmarked July 6, 1941....

"I'll marry you," she wrote....

That night I got up to the pulpit and preached. When I finished and sat down, the pastor turned to me.

"Do you know what you just said?" he asked.

"No," I confessed.

"I'm not sure the people did either."...

I raced right out and spent almost all of [the $165 honorarium] on an engagement ring with a diamond so big you could almost see it with a magnifying glass!...

"I can't wear the ring until I get permission from my parents," she said apologetically.

They were away, so she sent them a telegram: "Bill has offered me a ring. May I wear it?"

"Yes," they wired back, "if it fits."

Billy Graham, *Just As I Am*

Good of God

It was so very good of God to let my
      dreams come true,
to note a young girl's cherished hopes
then lead her right to you.

                    — Ruth Bell Graham,
                         Ruth: A Portrait

Diamonds in Your Backyard

A legend says that long ago in ancient Persia there lived a man named Ali Hafed. He owned a large farm filled with lush orchards, acres of grainfields, and beautiful gardens. His wife was lovely, and his children brought him great pleasure. Ali Hafed was quite content.

One day a sage came to visit. "Diamonds are to be desired above all else," the wizened old man told Ali, his eyes vibrant, his hands expressive. "If you have diamonds, you'll never want for anything."

The sage's words took root, and Ali became consumed with the translucent jewels—their fire, their depth, their worth. Soon Ali Hafed sold his farm and left his family to search the world for the finest diamonds. He would have them, no matter the cost.

Ali's quest took him all through Europe and down into Africa, but he found nothing that satisfied him. Before long, his money was gone, and his dreams of diamonds lay as shredded as the rags that clothed his body.

Hopeless and discouraged, Ali Hafed stood at the edge of a stormy Barbary Coast bay. Whipped by wind and rain, he stared at a giant tidal wave approaching the shore. But instead of running for safety, Ali calmly walked into the rolling surf and embraced the wave, ending his life.

The man who had purchased Ali Hafed's farm was watering his camel at the garden brook one day. The sun hung brilliant in the cloudless sky as the camel thrust his snout deep into the shallow water. Suddenly a bright glint in the white sand caught the farmer's eye. He bent down and gently brushed the sand away, revealing glistening stones. Diamonds. Scores and scores of diamonds.

There in the brook lay the beginnings of the most magnificent diamond mine in the history of humankind: the Golconda. From its depths would come the largest crown jewels in the world.

Ali Hafed had gone searching the world for diamonds, while all along, the largest and the very best lay under his feet.

The rarest, most beautiful diamonds are found in our own backyards. Don't run looking elsewhere. Take time to whisk away the sand that obscures your treasure. The sand of

For Denalyn, my wife: For making the grass so green on this side of the fence that the other side looks barren.

—MAX LUCADO, *A GENTLE THUNDER*

time and busyness. The silt of ingratitude. Let the water of forgiveness wash away the irritating granules of habit and personality that tend to rub the wrong way.

You'll discover diamonds. Scores and scores of diamonds. Right in your own backyard.

A wife of noble character who can find?
　　She is worth far more than rubies.
　　—Proverbs 31:10

Write out a brief blessing for your spouse and your marriage as you consider how you will strive to love each other well in the years ahead.

_____

_____

_____

_____

_____

_____

_____

_____

_____

_____

You are my husband.
My feet shall run because of you.
My feet dance because of you.
My heart shall beat because of you.
My eyes see because of you.
My mind thinks because of you.
And I shall love because of you.

—Eskimo love song

Rich Blessings

I wish you the blessing of God for a good beginning and
a steadfast middle time, and may you hold out until a
blessed end, this all in and through Jesus Christ. Amen.

Amish blessing

God, the best maker of all marriages,
Combine your hearts in one.

William Shakespeare

The LORD bless thee, and keep thee:
The LORD make his face shine upon thee, and be
    gracious unto thee:
The LORD lift up his countenance upon thee, and give
    thee peace.

Numbers 6:24–26, KJV

Sharing the Wealth

When John Palmer proposed to Debbie Clay back in the seventies, she knew she was in for a wild ride. Fresh out of college, John was pioneering a new church in Athens, Ohio, and had little to offer financially. But as sure as John was called to preach, Debbie felt called to be his wife…even though it meant living on sixty-four dollars a week.

The wedding was lovely.

Following the reception at Debbie's home church, the bride and groom drove toward Lansing, Michigan, and their first night together. A few miles out of town, John pulled over to the side of the road and shared his predicament. After scrimping and saving to pay for his groomsmen's tuxedos, John had very little money left for their honeymoon.

As he held her hands in his, he told his bride, "I've got tonight covered, but we only have a few dollars to make it up to Mackinaw Island." They had reservations at a small motel on the northern tip of Michigan and were looking forward to spending a few days relaxing in the cool waters where Lake Huron and Lake Michigan meet.

John reached into his tux's inner pocket and pulled out a bunch of cards he'd grabbed off the gift table before leaving the church. He held them up and said, "We get to go as far as we can with whatever people gave us."

One by one they opened the cards, carefully reading the sentiments before examining the contents. A ten-dollar bill dropped out of the first one and into Debbie's lap. "That'll get us to Saginaw!" A check here and a five there— like manna from heaven, the money drifted down, covering Debbie's lap and sliding onto the LeSabre's tan vinyl seats.

The honeymoon was everything they dreamed of and more.

When they returned to Athens to set up housekeeping, neither John nor Debbie had anything to fill the parsonage. Their possessions were few: some suitcases of clothing, a box of books from college, and assorted wedding gifts. But they were home. They nestled in with a borrowed table and two chairs and a mattress for the bedroom floor. The Lord had provided once. He would provide again.

Several weeks later, John's parents called to say they were going on the road. They didn't want to put their furniture in storage. Would John and Debbie mind keeping everything at their house?

Debbie motioned for John to come to the phone. Ear to ear they listened to the proposal, grinning and nodding at each other.

"Not at all, Mom," John said generously. "Not at all."

So do not worry, saying, "What shall we eat?" or "What shall we drink?" or "What shall we wear?" For the pagans run after all these things, and your heavenly Father knows that you need them. But seek first his kingdom and his righteousness, and all these things will be given to you as well.

—Matthew 6:31–33

My Wife

Trusty, dusky, vivid, true,
With eyes of gold and bramble-dew,
    Steel-true and blade-straight,
The great artificer
    Made my mate.

Honor, anger, valor, fire;
A love that life could never tire,
    Death quench or evil stir,
The mighty master
    Gave to her.

Teacher, tender comrade, wife,
A fellow-farer true through life,
    Heart-whole and soul-free
The august father
    Gave to me.

—Robert Louis Stevenson, from
Songs of Travel and Other Verses

My Husband

If ever two were one, then surely we.
If ever man were loved by wife, then thee;
If ever wife was happy in a man,
Compare with me, ye women, if you can.
I prize thy love more than whole mines
    of gold,
Or all the riches that the East doth hold.
My love is such that rivers cannot quench,
Nor ought but love from thee, give
    recompence.
Thy love is such that I can no way repay,
The heavens reward thee manifold, I pray.
Then while we live, in love let's so
    persevere,
That when we live no more, we may live
    ever.

—Anne Bradstreet, "To My Dear
    and Loving Husband"

I would rather have a crust and a tent with you than be
queen of all the world.

   Isabel Burton to her husband,
Sir Richard Burton

Having it all doesn't necessarily mean having it all
at once.

                    Stephanie Luetkehans

What special way (a secret code, a phrase, a touch, a look)
do you and your spouse express your love to each other that
is unknown to anyone except the two of you?

_____

_____

_____

_____

_____

_____

_____

_____

_____

_____

_____

_____

_____

_____

_____

_____

_____

_____

What does the symbolism of the wedding ring mean to you?

_____

_____

_____

_____

_____

_____

_____

_____

_____

_____

_____

_____

_____

_____

_____

_____

_____

_____

_____

What physical token of love other than your engagement
or wedding rings do you treasure? Why is it important
to you?

_____

_____

_____

_____

_____

_____

_____

_____

_____

_____

_____

_____

_____

_____

_____

_____

_____

_____

Part Five

The Declaration

*In the name of the Father, and of the Son,
and of the Holy Ghost. Amen. Those whom God
hath joined together, let no man put asunder.
Forasmuch as these two have consented together to
join in holy wedlock, I pronounce that they are
husband and wife. Amen. You may kiss your bride.*

Listen all ye that are present: Those that were distant are now brought together; those that were separated are now united."

In the Malacca Straits this is the proclamation the elder makes at the end of a marriage ceremony. Through the portal of these words, a couple embarks on a great adventure, filled with romance and intrigue. The proclamation marks the end of a wedding and the beginning of a marriage.

Jesus affirmed the sanctity of marriage when he echoed God's instruction to Adam and Eve in Genesis: " 'For this reason a man will leave his father and mother and be united to his wife, and the two will become one flesh.' So they are no longer two, but one. Therefore what God has joined together, let man not separate" (Matthew 19:5–6).

Like two children at a picnic, we as newlyweds are signed up for the three-legged race. Breathless with excitement and anticipation, we take our place at the starting line. "On your mark. Get set. Go!"

With the proclamation, we leave the altar, arm in arm. Together we begin to run, holding tightly to each other, lurching, laughing, lunging, and sometimes falling. But eventually we find the rhythm of being one, the smooth cadence of being husband and wife. And on we go, our eyes held fast to the goal, our hearts determined to reach the finish line one step at a time.

My fellow, my companion,
held most dear,
My soul, my other self,
my inward friend.

—MARY SIDNEY HERBERT

Shelter to the Other

Now we feel no rain, for each of us will
    be shelter to the other.
Now we will feel no cold, for each of us
    will be warmth to the other.
Now there is no loneliness for us.
Now we are two bodies, but only one life.
We go now to our dwelling place,
    to enter into the days of our togetherness.
May our days be good and long upon
    this earth.

—Apache blessing

Sealing the Agreement

Ah, the kiss. What could be more romantic? Adolescent hearts tremble and poets' pens fill pages—all in tribute to this tiny but fiercely emotional act. What is it about the anatomical juxtaposition of two orbicularis oris muscles in the state of contraction that causes old women to blush and turns grown men to mush?

We could discuss the chemical effects of endorphins and adrenaline upon the body. We might speak of Dr. Freud or the favorable impact of Tic Tacs on the art of smooching, but I think it's much simpler than that. And much more mysterious.

Besides food, water, and shelter, touch remains one of our greatest human needs. Somehow in touching we connect. And when we connect, we understand and are understood. And somewhere in the understanding, we know we are loved.

There is something sacred about two souls intentionally meeting at the point of all breath and life. The Bible speaks of the passionate kiss only three times (Proverbs 7:13; Song of Songs 1:2; 8:1). More common was the platonic kiss, used as a symbol of reverence and respect. Perhaps that is why the early Christians adopted the kiss as holy, giving it near sacramental importance.

Throughout history and civilizations, a kiss sealed covenants and marked legal agreements. Many government leaders take their oaths of office by kissing the Bible, thus pledging fidelity. In marital history, the courtship could be called off at any time before the betrothal kiss, but as soon as the two pairs of lips met, the marriage was confirmed both legally and socially.

The kiss was so binding in Italy at one time that if a maiden was kissed by a young man in public, they had to get married. In Venice, young women of the wealthier classes actually wore long, white veils and required armed escorts to protect them from unwanted admirers.

How appropriate, how blessed, the kiss becomes when exchanged at the end of the marriage ceremony. Mixed with passion, reverence, and respect, it seals with a benediction all that has been promised. Like a stamp on a long letter filled with dreams and words of love, the kiss sends us on our way. There is no possibility of retrieving the letter or turning back.

The postage has been paid and our matrimonial envelope sealed with a kiss. And neither snow nor rain nor heat nor gloom of night shall keep us from our appointed duty.

Let him kiss me with the kisses of his mouth—
   for your love is more delightful than wine.
   —Song of Songs 1:2

What's in

A kiss, when all is said, what is it?
An oath that's given closer than before;
A promise more precise; the sealing of
Confessions that till then were barely breathed;
A rosy dot placed on the "i" in loving.

— Edmond Rostand, *Cyrano de Bergerac*

I bless you. I kiss and caress every tenderly beloved
place and gaze into your deep, sweet eyes which long
ago conquered me completely. Love ever grows.

— Alexandra to Czar Nicholas II of Russia

a Kiss?

Already the second day since our marriage, his love and gentleness is beyond everything, and to kiss that dear soft cheek, to press my lips to his, is heavenly bliss. I feel a purer more unearthly feel than I ever did. Oh! was ever a woman so blessed as I am.

Queen Victoria, journal entry, February 12, 1840

Four sweet lips, two pure souls, and one undying affection—these are love's pretty ingredients for a kiss.

Christian N. Bovee

First Kiss

It was a kiss that woke Sleeping Beauty. It was a kiss that freed Snow White from a jealous queen's poison. And it was a kiss that sealed the true-life fairy-tale romance of Gwendylann and Stone Faulkenberry.

But these two saved the best for last.

While Prince Charming began his courtship with a kiss, Stone was determined to do things differently with Gwendylann. In the past, Stone's relationships had left a trail of shame and broken hearts.

"I've made a covenant with the Lord that I won't kiss a woman until I kiss my bride on our wedding day," Stone told Gwendylann a few weeks after they started seeing each other. "Unless you're willing to make the same covenant, I can't see you anymore."

Gwen agreed. The next six months were filled with picnics, flying kites, and chocolate frozen yogurt. Slowly they opened their lives to each other through hours of talking but rarely touching. Postponing the physical part of their relationship created a deep friendship. And then a romance.

One warm August evening as they sat beside a tranquil lake, Stone Faulkenberry told Gwendylann Ford, "I love you." There were no games. They both knew what the words implied. When Gwen had agreed to no kissing, she'd included an addendum. "Don't tell me you love me until you mean it forever," she had said, as serious about her request as he was about his. "I've heard those words before, and they were empty and cheap."

That October they were engaged. In December, their pastor pronounced them man and wife. "You may kiss your bride...."

As Stone lifted Gwen's veil, it was more than symbolic. He had covenanted to present his wife to the Lord, holy and blameless, without stain or wrinkle according to Ephesians 5:27. And that's what he did. "I don't want to add or take anything away from you," he'd told Gwen early on.

The kiss was everything they had waited for and more. "Honoring and pure," Gwendylann says in her soft southern accent. "Like all of God's best wrapped into one little kiss."

*Love is not a matter of
counting the years;
it is making the years count.*

—WILLIAM SMITH

After the pronouncement they ran down the aisle and into the foyer. "It was so much fun!" Gwen says with a shimmering giggle. "We just kissed and kissed—'cause we could!"

Now after six years of marriage, Stone and Gwen still find value in the simple joys of love. Holding hands. A tender kiss. A meaning-filled glance. Walking side by side, their shoulders brushing, their lives entwined.

For those who haven't lived a fairy-tale, Gwen and Stone believe in new beginnings. "We can throw ourselves on God's mercy and know He forgives. He delights to restore. It's never too late to set up a milestone and say, 'From here on…'

"It's not so much how you start—it's how you finish," Gwen says. Then smiling at her own Prince Charming, she adds:

"God loves happy endings!"

Write a brief letter to your spouse about how you feel as
you anticipate the rest of your life together.

_____

_____

_____

_____

_____

_____

_____

_____

_____

_____

Near in My Heart

My greatest good fortune in a life of brilliant
experiences has been to find you, and to
lead my life with you. I don't feel far away
from you out here at all. I feel very near in
my heart; and also I feel that the nearer
I get to honour, the nearer I am to you.

—Winston Churchill, in a letter to his wife

Forever and Always

Of all the strange places for love to show up. Cupid on his worst day would have had enough sense to point his bow elsewhere.

She was a direct descendant of Jonathan Edwards, the great preacher. He was a rough-and-tumble cowboy who'd left home at twelve years of age to bust broncos. She was quiet. He was loud and boisterous. Definitely opposites. And attract they did.

When Ray Weaver caught a glimpse of Rena Edwards, the local preacher's daughter, he knew he would marry her. It was the start of a love affair that lasted over six decades.

I saw the depth of this unlikely love one April evening over wieners and sauerkraut. Newly engaged to their grandson John, I looked forward to meeting the couple that had so influenced his life.

At ninety years of age, Grandpa had been caring for his paralyzed sweetheart for over three years. A stroke had completely silenced the quiet woman, leaving her paralyzed with only her eyes and one curled fist for communicating.

"She's taken care of me for over sixty years," Grandpa informed the family when they'd initially suggested a nursing home. "God's given me this chance to minister to her, and I ain't gonna miss it."

It hadn't been easy.

The hot dogs were cold in the middle and the sauerkraut lukewarm, but we feasted on Grandpa's cuisine and dry humor. Grandma's pale blue eyes sparked as she looked from her lover to her grandson while they bantered back and forth. Now and then Grandpa reached over and put his huge spotted hand over her tiny curled one, patting it gently as he told another whopper.

When Grandma passed away the next year, Grandpa was lost. He didn't want to be a burden to anyone. His two sons took him on a trip back to the old homestead in Nebraska and to Wyoming to see where he broke broncos.

It was there that Grandpa got his lifelong wish. He'd always said if he didn't go in the Rapture, he wanted to die in Wyoming with his boots on. Three weeks after his dear Rena went to be with Jesus, Ray Weaver died just outside of Douglas, Wyoming. With his boots on.

I can just imagine him standing at the pearly gates, holding on to his beautiful wife with one hand, the dusty old cowboy hat he always wore with the other. And after three years of silence, I wouldn't be surprised if the first words out of his sweetheart's lips were, "Ray, wipe those feet. You're messing up the streets of gold!"

"Under the Harvest Moon"

Under the summer roses
When the flagrant crimson
Lurks in the dusk
Of the wild red leaves,
Love, with little hands,
Comes and touches you
With a thousand memories,
And asks you
Beautiful, unanswerable questions.

—Carl Sandburg

Two Become One

They sat side by side in the dark, holding hands. My husband, John, didn't see them until he flipped on the switch, filling the prayer room with light.

"I'm sorry," John said. "I didn't think anyone was in here."

"Not a problem," the old gentleman said with a wink. The two sat close at one end of a pew that stretched along the far wall. He gathered his tiny, gray-haired wife a bit closer, and she smiled shyly, looking at her husband and then at the embarrassed youth pastor. John stood there for a moment, uncertain.

He'd heard about the old man, how he had once been a strapping young farmer, tilling the fields of eastern Montana from dawn till dusk. But now his body was bent and grizzled, the large ranch abandoned years ago for a small house in town. His wife fit neatly beneath his arm as each Sunday they shook John's hand after morning service.

Like two puzzle pieces they fit. Like two shadows melded into a single silhouette. Differences had long ago been blended by compromise, their original diversity somehow faded into the sweet unity of many loving years. They even looked alike, their features softened by age to a near sibling-like sameness.

John came home that night and shared the story. "I want a love like that," John said, his voice tender with emotion. Our lives had grown so busy we'd barely had time for each other. Together we prayed, asking God to help us build a love that years could not put asunder. Asking that he would make us truly one. Asking that when we grew old and gray, we'd not only resemble each other, but we'd still find time to hold hands in the dark.

John chuckled as he told me how the couple had exchanged pleasantries with him after he'd interrupted them, but at the first lull in the conversation, the old Scandinavian farmer released John politely, saying, "You can go now."

"Of course," John stuttered, backing out the door.

"Oh—and, Pastor?" the farmer said, smiling mischievously. "Don't forget to turn off the light."

So they are no longer two, but one. Therefore what God has joined together, let man not separate.
    —Matthew 19:6

So we grew together,

Like to a double cherry, seeming parted,

But yet an union in partition;

Two lovely berries moulded on one stem.

William Shakespeare,
A Midsummer Night's Dream

Two souls with but a single thought,

Two hearts that beat as one.

Eligius von Münch-Bellinghausen

It is the man and woman united that make the complete human being. Separate, she lacks his force of body and strength of reason; he, her softness, sensibility, and acute discernment. Together they are more likely to succeed in the world.

— Benjamin Franklin

I think a man and woman should choose each other for life, for the simple reason that a long life is barely enough for a man and woman to understand each other; and to understand is to love.

— J. B. Yeats

What do you remember about your first kiss with your spouse?

_____

_____

_____

_____

_____

_____

_____

_____

_____

_____

_____

_____

_____

_____

_____

_____

_____

_____

_____

What has helped you and your spouse grow closer together since the time you met?

Imagine you have been married fifty years—and maybe you have! What is the one most significant thing you would like to be able to say about your marriage?

_____

_____

_____

_____

_____

_____

_____

_____

_____

_____

_____

_____

_____

_____

_____

_____

_____

_____

_____

I Do Love You

I do love you...as the dew loves the flowers; as the birds love the sunshine; as the wavelets love the breeze; as mothers love their firstborn; as memory loves old faces; as the yearning tides love the moon; as the angels love the pure in heart.

— Samuel Clemens (Mark Twain)
in a letter to Olivia Langdon, 1869

A successful marriage requires falling in love many times, always with the same person.

— Mignon McLaughlin

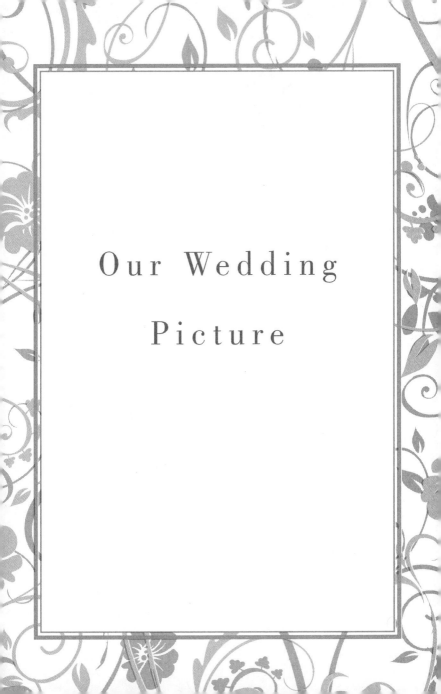

Our Wedding

Picture

Bride's Personal Vows

Record the vows you made at your wedding.

_____

_____

_____

_____

_____

_____

_____

_____

_____

_____

_____

_____

_____

_____

_____

_____

_____

_____

_____

_____

 Personal Vows

Record the vows you made at your wedding.

_____

_____

_____

_____

_____

_____

_____

_____

_____

_____

_____

_____

_____

_____

_____

_____

_____

_____

_____

_____

_____

_____

Never, never, never, never give up.

—Winston Churchill

Sources

Part One

12 Robert Creeley, "Love Comes Quietly," in *The Collected Poems of Robert Creeley, 1945–1975* (Berkeley: University of California Press, 1983), 249. Copyright © 1983 by the Regents of the University of California. Used by permission.

18 Michael C. Blumenthal, "A Marriage," in *Against Romance* (New York: Viking-Penguin, 1987), 16. Used by permission of the author.

23 Paul Valéry, "My Life Has Been…," in *Poems in the Rough,* Bollingen Series 45, vol. 2, *The Collected Works in English,* trans. Hilary Corke (Princeton, NJ: Princeton University Press, 1969). Copyright © 1969 by Princeton University Press, copyright renewed 1997 by Princeton University Press. Used by permission.

Part Two

33 "Come What May" told with the permission of Kim and Krickitt Carpenter, who tell their full story in *The Vow: The Kim and Krickitt Carpenter Story* (Nashville: Broadman & Holman, 2000). Used by permission.

42 "A Dream Come True" told with the permission of Jim and Patty Porter.

Part Three

72 "Let Me Be Your Mirror" adapted from Bill and Pam Farrel, *Love to Love You: Creating Romantic Moments Together* (Eugene, OR: Harvest House, 1997), 12.

Part Four

86 "I got a thick letter…," Billy Graham, *Just As I Am* (New York: HarperCollins, 1997), 75–76.

87 "It was so very good…," Ruth Graham, *Ruth: A Portrait* (New York: Doubleday, 1997), 87. Used by permission.

89 "Sharing the Wealth" told with the permission of John and Debbie Palmer.

Part Five

110 "First Kiss" told with the permission of Stone and Gwendylann Faulkenberry.

About the Author

JOANNA WEAVER is the author of the best-selling books *Having a Mary Heart in a Martha World* and *Having a Mary Spirit*.

Joanna and her husband, John, have been married more than twenty-six years and have three children. She and John want you to know, "it just gets sweeter and sweeter!"